A Step-by-Step Guide to

Rediscovering

HOPE

(<u>H</u>ISTORICALLY <u>O</u>NE-SIZED <u>P</u>ROVEN <u>E</u>CONOMICAL)
Classic Cloth Diapers

Amy McKnight

The information in this booklet is true to the best of the author's knowledge and her ability to relate it. While the author has endeavored to present the content accurately and honestly, the author disclaims any responsibility or liability for errors, omissions, or the accuracy or reliability of the information presented. By using the information herein, you assume all risks associated with the use thereof. The author shall not in any event be liable for any direct, indirect, punitive, special, incidental, or consequential damages, including and without limitations, lost revenues or lost profits arising out of or in any way connected with the use of this material.

VELCRO* is the name of a hook and loop fastener and is a trademark of Velcro Industries.

Contents

Introduction

(How I Found HOPE)

According to a study published in The Journal of Pediatrics in July 2013, one in three American mothers live in a hopeless situation, without enough diapers to change her child. I learned about this when my husband and I were starting a family and getting ready for our new addition.

I came across an online article entitled, "High Cost of Diapers Forces Some Parents into Risky Practices ." It shared what some mothers had to do to "stretch diapers." The article bothered me enough to make me want to do something.

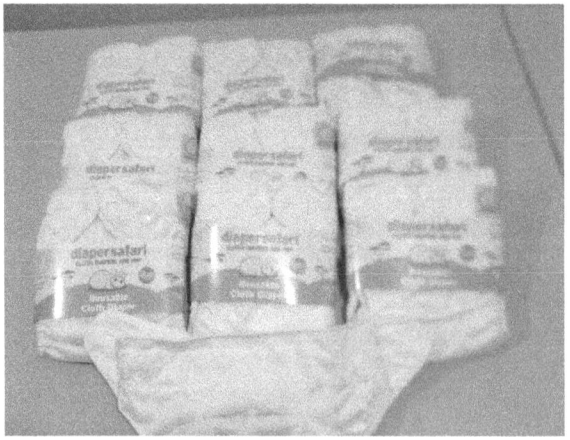

I had already researched and purchased a starter set of pocket cloth diapers, and they were on their way to me in the mail. As I see it, using cloth diapers is about being a good steward of the environment and saving money. When I looked at the problems facing mothers looking for creative ways to make ends meet, it seemed cloth diapers might be the answer for the problems for the mothers in the article as well. Still, I could see how the usual startup cost might be beyond the means of the families who most needed to use cloth diapers. I realized if I wanted to help, I'd need to find a solution that could work for mothers in the greatest need as well as mothers like me who had other options.

I sent back the diapers I had ordered and jumped in the deep end, on a mission to find a sustainable solution—one I could use with my own baby and one I could pass along as a viable option for anyone open to cloth diapering, not just those who were struggling to make ends meet. It had to be accessible to the widest range of people and work for any budget.

I spent a good part of my pregnancy researching a variety of diapering options. I created a pattern for adjustable one-size fits most diapers made from t-shirts, that was very easy to make for even the most basic sewer. The problem of diaper need was constantly on my mind, and there was one answer that seemed to come up time and time again: Use classic cloth diapers. Still, I

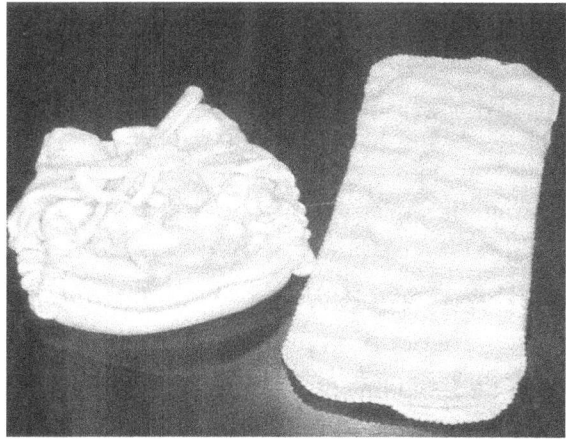

kept writing that off. It just seemed so old-fashioned and inconvenient!

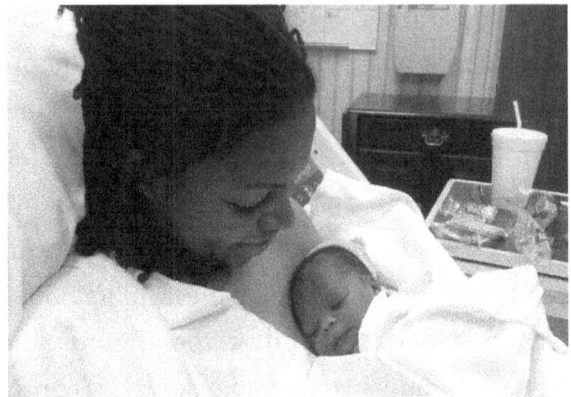

On the day our daughter was born, I was forced to consider classic diapers, a tiny 6.7-pound bundle of joy. The t-shirt diapers I had so carefully made for her didn't fit, so the pattern would have to be tweaked, albeit at a later date.

I had purchased and prepared flour sack towels (the original classic cloth diapers) to go into the t-shirt diapers to make them more absorbent, so I had flour sack towels with me at the hospital. I quickly gave myself a crash course in folding classic cloth diapers for newborns.

From the day our daughter was born, we used classic diapers. I was torn about that. After all, I'd spent over a year of my life working on my easy-to-make t-shirt diaper pattern, but we actually used classic diapers.

Then it hit me. I was living what I had wanted to do. I had found an easy solution that was good enough for my own daughter, and I could honestly tell other mothers, "You can do this! It's what I'm doing, and it works." Just like that, while looking for a solution everywhere but right in front of me, I'd found HOPE!

In order to keep a baby dry, a caregiver needs an adequate

supply of diapers; it isn't healthy to leave a child in a wet or messy diaper. In the current market, three days' worth of classic cloth diapers (about 36 or more flat cloths for diapers and 4 moisture-proof covers) can be purchased for the cost of a month's supply of disposables or as much as $350. Classic cloth diapers are truly the great equalizer, and there is a classic style diaper for every budget.

My goal is to share what I've learned and how I've come to adore classic diapering. I've found HOPE, for myself, for mothers in need, and for a greener tomorrow.

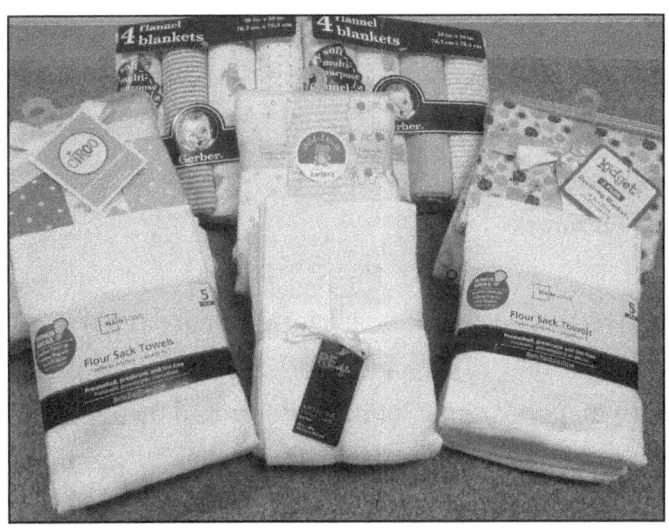

Seven Reasons to Consider Cloth

"Why would anyone choose to diaper their baby in cloth diapers in the first place?"

It's a very good question and one I am often asked. Here are seven reasons to consider using cloth as an alternative to disposables:

1. The Health Factor
2. The Environmental Impact
3. The Financial Benefits
4. The Ease of Use
5. The Effectiveness
6. The Convenience
7. The Cuteness

The Health Factor

In general, babies who wear cloth diapers suffer from fewer incidents of diaper rash than children who wear disposables. In fact, cloth diapers are sometimes prescribed by pediatricians for children suffering from severe rash or allergic reactions to the materials used to produce disposable diapers.

Ever wonder why some disposable diapers can hold ten or more pees? They are manufactured with a chemical cocktail that keeps babies from feeling wet, but even if your little one does not feel it, the soft skin of their little bottom is still sitting in pee.

Babies who wear cloth diapers also tend to potty train sooner. It is thought that this is due to earlier understanding of cause and effect, because when a little one uses the bathroom, they feel it right away. It could also be because parents who cloth diaper tend to pay more attention to their babies' toileting cues and change their children more often, also reinforcing cause and effect.

Finally, an often overlooked health factor is that of the mental health of parents. Even off-brand disposables are a hefty expense, and when parents don't have enough diapers, they are forced to ration what they do have. This can lead to skin infections, diaper rash, and generally fussy babies. It is heartwrenching for parents to see their child suffering and uncomfortable and to be unable to meet that child's needs, and feelings of guilt and inadequacy can impact parents a great deal. Reusable cloth diapers allow parents to wash and reuse diapers, thus reducing parents' mental and emotional stress.

The Environmental Impact

No one really knows how long it will take for all of the disposable diapers in the landfills to biodegrade, but it is estimated that it will take between 250 to 500 years. In the meantime, dirty diapers are decaying in our landfills, and polluting our ground water. In addition, trees that would help rid our air harmful CO_2 emissions are being cut down and used as wood pulp to make disposables.

Most cloth diapers are made of easily biodegradable natural fibers. Cloth diapers are generally used multiple times, sometimes with multiple children before finally being downgraded to rags or thrown away.

Just as important, the majority of the poop from a cloth diaper is either flushed down the toilet or washed down the drain. In this way, the human body waste is treated as it should be – in the septic, sewer, or water treatment system instead of lying in landfills to spread sickness and disease.

The Financial Benefits

Disposable diapers are costly in many ways beyond financial. They are costly to children's health and to our environment. However, the impact on a family's budget can also be astronomical, especially for those struggling in a relatively unstable economy. A family can spend anywhere from $1,500 for off-brand diapers to $4,000 for "eco-friendly" disposable diapers from birth to potty training. Convenience is the only return on investment.

Cloth diapers can have upfront cost of as little as $100 or up to $1,000 . Even if one went all out and got the super-duper patented poop collectors, there would still be a minimum savings of $500 for the first child, and since diapers can be reused for other babies, the savings would only compound for each additional child. Cloth diapers are an investment, a fixed cost rather than an ongoing expense.

The Ease of Use

Using cloth diapers isn't inherently complicated; it can be as complicated or simple as you make it. Most of them are worn much like disposables. Flushable liners can be used for those who are squeamish, and there is absolutely no need to rinse them in the toilet or have them sitting in standing water.

New innovations like the Snappi, a modern alternative to diaper pins, make even the most basic types of cloth diapers easy to use. Aside from a few extra loads of laundry and some extra folding/stuffing, they perform the same job as a disposable—only over and over and over again.

The Effectiveness

Cloth diapers work, period. Parents who switch from disposables to cloth, especially during the runny poop stage, find that up -the-back blowouts are a thing of the past. Thanks to elastic in the waist and legs, cloth diapers and diaper covers keep the mess where it belongs: in the diaper instead of on the baby's clothes, the furniture, or you.

The Convenience

No matter what your financial situation, it is a whole lot more convenient to do a load of laundry every three to four days than it is to make a run to the store for disposable diapers at four a.m. Diapers can be washed and ready to go, leaving busy parents time to take care of other things.

Even if you have to hand wash diapers, it a lot easier to wash twice a week than to work extra hours, find another job, or to helplessly listen to a suffering baby cry because she's in a dirty diaper.

The Cute Factor

There's something about cloth diapers that make many parents smile. Maybe it's the wide variety of prints, colors, and patterns. Maybe it's the fluffy little bottoms. Whatever it is, cloth diapers are just downright cute!

Now that we've examined the general advantages of cloth diapers, let's explore one particular type that affords all of the benefits mentioned above in addition to a couple more.

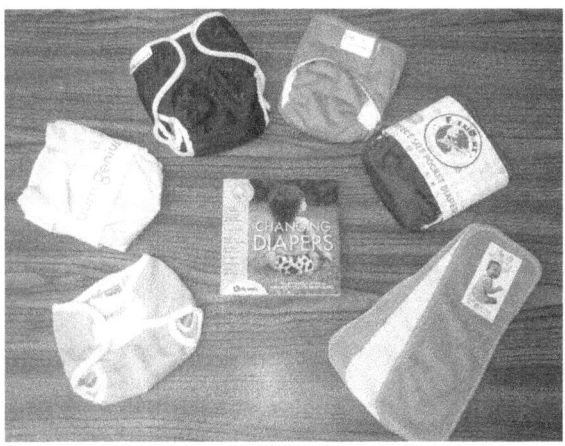

Classic Diapers Equal HOPE

What is HOPE?

As the world changes, grows, and seems to become more cynical and difficult and crowded and confusing by the day, hope has become harder and harder to find, even for well-educated people. Our environment is being destroyed by petrochemicals and trash that may never biodegrade, and, frankly, it isn't the prettiest world to bring a baby into.

Whether you choose cloth diapers to save green or because you want to go green, there is hope for families with babies, hope for a better brighter future. As I pondered this, I realized that HOPE can serve as an acronym for one of the most amazing rediscoveries of the twenty-first century: the classic flat cloth diaper. Classic flat cloth diapers offer HOPE because they are:

Historically
One-Sized
Proven
Economical (Eco-Friendly and Easier to Use Than You Think!)

Historically

Classic flat cloth diapers have been around for a very long time. The word diaper actually refers to the diamond-shaped pattern woven into the cotton or linen used for diapering.

Around the 1600s, diaper began to refer to the actual article of clothing.

From 1800 to the middle of last century, foods such as flour, cornmeal, and sugar came in 50- or 100-pound cotton sacks. Families couldn't afford to waste anything, so those sacks were often cut up to make clothing, bedding, towels, and diapers for babies.

In general, classic diapers—flour sack towels in particular—have stood the test of time as cloth diapers.

One-Sized

A twenty-seven-by-twenty-seven-inch square of cotton cloth can be folded to fit a tiny newborn. That same square of cloth can be combined with another and folded to fit a toddler. How's that for transformability? No more leaks due to baby being between sizes!

Proven

The fact that flat cloth diapers are classic diapers isn't enough to prove how wonderful they are. However, after 400-plus years, more than a few post-modern mothers are still using them, and that speaks volumes!

Economical

Almost any 100 percent cotton square of cloth can be used as a classic flat diaper. Flannel receiving blankets work amazingly well, especial for older children and overnight.

Take a moment and think outside the box, and you'll realize you have a lot of available options for classic diapers.

Although 100 percent cotton is the most widely available type of commercial classic flat diapers, there are high-end choices, even in the world of flat cloth diapers. Think organic hemp or bamboo. You can diaper in classic flat cloth diapers and still keep your posh-posh card!

These modern blends will keep Junior's bottom exceptionally dry without looking too cheap. At around seven dollars per flat square, these are definitely not your grandmother's flour sack diapers.

Eco-Friendly

Cloth diapering is, in general, better for the environment, and classic flat cloth diapers are exceptionally so, as they are amazingly easy to wash and they dry quickly.

One of the reasons I personally adore classic flat cloth diapers is that they offer the most uses out of a single item. I use my flat diapers as diapers, burp cloths, nursing covers, swaddling blankets, sunshields, changing mats, and the list could go on. After I'm done diapering, it is an inherently wonderful way to cut down on a large percentage of paper towel usage.

Easier Than You Think

I'll be honest: When I first heard about using flat cloths as diapers, I was not excited about the thought. However, before long, I realized it was as easy as folding any other article of clothing. Once they are folded, using them is a breeze.

Over the months, through research and trial and error, I've created a system of washing, drying, and folding diapers that really makes using classic flat cloth diapers no big deal. Let me show you why I belive classic diapers are the ideal solution for diapering needs, as well as a means of creating a greener tomorrow.

What You'll Need – (And Why)

Here is a list of the basic things you'll need to diaper successfully with classic flat cloth diapers. There are explanations of each below.

- 36 to 70 flat cloths
- 36 to 70 fleece liners
- 36 to 90 cloth wipes
- 4 to 8 diaper covers
- 1 to 2 Snappis or 2 to 3 sets of pins
- A diaper pail/large trashcan
- A wet/wet-dry bag
- Cloth-friendly detergent
- 4 to 6 pocket diapers (optional)
- Breathing mobile washer (optional)

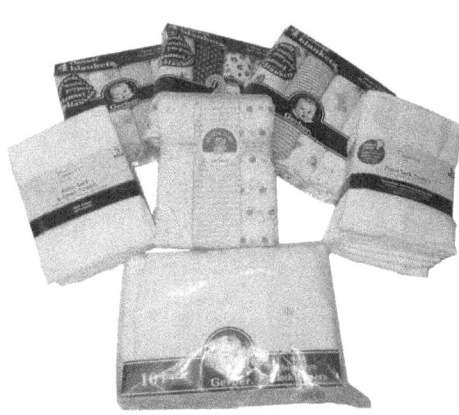

Flat Cloths

You'll need 36 to 70 flat cloths, enough that you'll have some clean and ready for use while the others are in the wash twice a week, every 3 to 4 days. Almost any 100 percent cotton material will work. It should be about 27"x27" to 30"x30" inches; for diapers that will supply your baby from birth to potty training, you won't want to go much smaller or bigger than that.

Types of Classic Flat Cloth Diapers

Gerber flats cost more than flour sack towels, shrink down to only about 23" to 25" square after they are washed, and really don't absorb as much or as well as flour sacks or receiving blankets. However, if you have a super tiny baby, they could work for you. They can also be used to add absorbency when your baby wets too much for one flour sack but not enough to warrant using two.

Flour sack towels are generally the cheapest option, as well as the most versatile. As your baby grows and begins to wet more, you can double them, especially during nights and naps. They are readily available in the kitchen and dining section of most big-box stores.

Flannel receiving blankets add fun to classic diapering. They come in a wide variety of prints. You can use them for naps and nights because they hold a lot before getting soaked, and they make it easy to know which diaper to grab.

Fleece Liners

The world of classic diapering is a lot more comfortable for baby and less messy for parents these days, thanks to fleece liners, which serve basically two purposes: They catch the majority of the poop and keep your baby's bottom dry by serving as a barrier between the skin and the wet diaper. You can wash the poopy liners separately from the rest of your diaper wash. This is a plus, whether you are washing by hand or in a machine.

If you decided to use fleece liners, you'll need a liner for each diaper. You can purchase commercially made ones for about a dollar each, or you can buy dollar store fleece receiving blankets and cut them into eighths or twelfths.

Diaper Fasteners

There are two popular types of diaper fasteners, the Snappi and tried-and-true diaper pins.

The Snappi

The Snappi is a three-armed device with little claws at the end of each arm. You hook left right and center (right left and center if you are left-handed) to hold the diaper in place. The Snappi should only be used under a diaper cover of some sort, as little fingers could easily pull it off.

Diaper Pins

Then there are the faithful diaper pins. They aren't as flashy as Snappis, but they get the job done. With a little practice, they are not that hard to use. If you are using pins, be sure to buy those specifically made for diapers; they have special locking heads that make it hard, if not impossible, for little fingers to open them.

If you want to let your little one walk around without a diaper cover on, you'll need to use pins; otherwise, you'll have a naked baby and possibly a trail of mess to clean up!

Whichever fastener you choose, be sure you have a couple of sets.

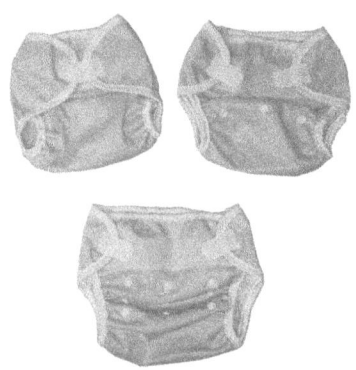

Diaper Covers

One size fits most Velcro diaper covers are the easiest to use. Most will work from seven to thirty-five pounds. The key is the cross-over Velcro. You'll generally only use two to three covers a day. This is because most changes are pee, and the diapers are rarely drenched. If you fold the diapers so that they properly wrap around your child's bottom, you can protect the cover from poop. You can definitely survive with four if you wash covers be-tween the times you do laundry, but six to eight is best.

Cloth Baby Wipes

Since you are already going to be washing diapers, adding wipes to the wash won't be a problem, and it can save you a good deal of money. You can purchase commercial cloth wipes for one to two dollars, baby washcloths for twenty-five to seventy-five cents, or make your own from upcycled materials for close to nothing. If you want to use cloth wipes exclusively, you'll need about one to two wipes per diaper change.

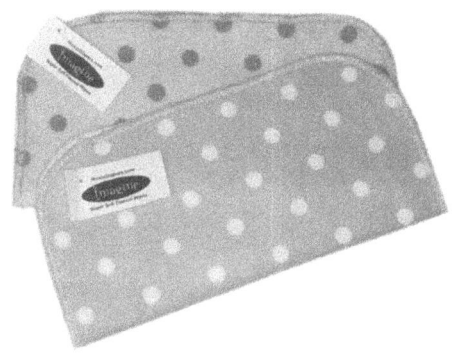

A Wet/Wet-Dry Bag

This is how you will store your diapers when you are out and about. A wet bag is a single-compartment, waterproof bag that holds a set amount of soiled diapers. A wet-dry bag has two compartments, one for clean diaper and one for soiled.

Diaper Pail/Large Trashcan

You'll need to store your soiled diapers somewhere until wash day. A larger kitchen trashcan with a spring-loaded lid can hold about three days' worth of diapers. When it starts getting high, you know it's time to make time to wash.

You can rinse the can on laundry day and not bother with diaper pail liners, or you can purchase those to go in your diaper pail/trashcan or to use as a standalone method of holding your diapers.

Four to Six Pocket Diaper Shells

You and the significant other may be on the same page about cloth diapering, but Grandma may not be too keen on the two-part diaper system, and the daycare down the street can't use your covers more than once. (Yes, there are daycares that will take children with cloth, but we'll discuss that more later.)

In such cases, you'll need to provide them with something that is easier for them to use. There pocket diapers shells just hold the cloth in place. You just pad fold the flat cloth and stuff it into the pocket where the inserts would go. They have a fleece stay dry layer, to keep your little one's bottom dry.

Breathing Mobile Washer

When looking for a solution for the problem of how to wash a diaper when one doesn't have a washing machine, I came across this amazing little device that has been used around the world, the Breathing Mobile Washer, a manual clothes washer that pushes and pulls water through fabrics.

It looks like a plunger, but it is made from hard material and will provide you with many years of use. You don't need to use a lot of water, yet it cleans diapers as well, if not better than my HE washing machine. I use it to pre-wash poopy liners and to wash my main diaper load when washing by hand.

Cloth-Friendly Detergent

Here is another beautiful thing about 100 percent cotton classic flat cloth diapers: They are really forgiving. Yes, there are some guidelines as to what detergents you should and should not use, but you really can use brands you can find locally. The problem with most cloth diapers and mainstream detergent, as far as I can tell, is buildup.

If you only have, say, twenty-four diapers, you have to wash all of them every day and a half to two days, and that can cause a great deal of detergent buildup. If you have fifty to seventy diapers in your stash, you won't have to wash the same diaper more than once or twice a week. You will also be less tempted to leave your child in a diaper to "get an extra pee," which just saturates the diapers, forcing you to use more detergent and water to get them clean.

Give HOPE

Here's what you can do to spread the word about *Rediscovering HOPE*:

1. Please like this book on Facebook www.facebook.com/HOPEDiapers

2. Please tweet about it on Twitter #HOPEDiapers

3. Send links to the download Rediscovering.HOPEDiapers.org

4. Consider purchasing copies of the informational brochure edition of this book for local charities, community service, family aid group at: http://hopediapers.org/get-booklets

Initial

Preparations

Out of the package, no new cloth diaper is ready to use. All must go through a basic prepping process so they will hold more liquid.

There are two methods of doing this. First, you can put them through several rounds of washing and drying. Or, you can boil them. Let's look at how to do both, and then I'll explain the method I use and why.

Prepping by Washing

If you have purchased thirty-six or more flat cloths and want to prep them all at once and have ready access to a washer and dryer, this may be the best method for you.

1. Put the flat cloths into the machine.

2. Add one-quarter of the amount of your cloth-friendly detergent. (See the washing section for list.)

3. Run a hot wash.

4. Place diapers in the dryer and dry.

5. Repeat Steps 1 thorough 4 two to three more times.

6. Pour some water on them. It should be absorbed quickly. If it beads up and doesn't absorb, you may have used too much or the wrong type of detergent. (See troubleshooting section.)

Prepping by Boiling

If you are prepping a few diapers at a time or if, for whatever reason, you don't have access to a washing machine (traveling, camping, etc.), this method may work very well for you.

1. Use a large stockpot, such as the kind used to make soup or pasta for a large crowd.

2. Fill the pot two-thirds of the way full with water. Add a drop or two of blue Dawn dish detergent.

3. Place on the stove on medium-high and bring it to a boil.

4. Add diapers to the water one at a time. Five seem to fit well in my largest pot.

5. Let them simmer for about fifteen to twenty minutes, stirring from time to time or pushing them under if they try to bubble up.

6. Get out a strainer and bowl and serving tongs.

7. Carefully remove diapers one by one with serving tongs and place them in a strainer over the larger bowl. Add more water to the pot and bring to a boil again.

8. Repeat Steps 2 through 7, until you've boiled all diapers.

9. Let diapers cool. It may take a while, and **those on the bottom and in the center will be hot; be careful!**

10. Wring out the diapers and hang them over a drying rack,

on a line, or on an octopus rack to dry. If you have access to a washing machine and dryer and enough diapers to justify turning the washer on, put them in the washer on the drain/spin cycle and spin them dry. Then toss them in the dryer.

The Method I Use

I use the boiling method to prep my diapers. I've only used the washing method once, the first time to prep about twenty diapers. I have close to 100 diapers, most of which were prepped on the stove. I find it is faster and seems to use less energy for the same results.

Your diapers will become more absorbent with time and will reach their peak absorbency after six washes. If you aren't rationing diapers, you shouldn't need them to absorb Niagara Falls! If you change your child every one to two hours for newborns and infants and every couple of hours and when you know they've pooped for older children, you should be fine.

- **ONLY prep/ boil** the actual flat cloth that will be used for diapers (flour sack towels, receiving blankets, etc.)

- **DO NOT boil** the diaper covers! This will cause the water proofing layer to deteriorate and lead to leaks.

Using Your Diapers

In this chapter, you'll learn how to size your diaper cover and pocket diapers and how to put on an already-folded diaper with a cover. We will cover folding in the next chapter.

Sizing Your Cover

One-size-fits-most diaper covers fit babies between seven and thirty-five pounds. The sizes are adjustable to three different sizes, by adjusting the front snaps you can change the size of the leg opening and the distance from the crotch to the waist in the front, from small to medium to larger.

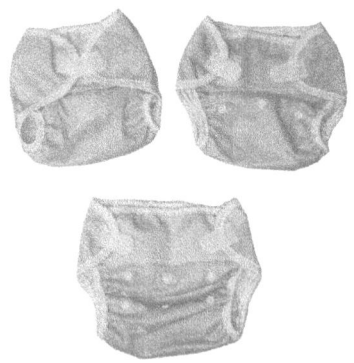

• To make the smallest-sized diaper cover, snap the top row of male/stud snaps to the bottom row of female/socket snaps.

• To make the medium-sized diaper cover, snap the top row of male/stud snaps to the middle row of female/socket snaps.

• To make use the diaper cover at its largest size, open all the snaps.

• The waist is adjusted much like disposables, with Velcro tabs.

• The diaper should be snug, without pinching or leaving red marks. You should be able to get a finger under the waist and in the leg openings when the diaper is on your child.

How to Use
Pocket Diapers

Pocket diapers can be used by childcare providers, Daddy, or Grandma, but are also easy to wash for those who have no other choice but to wash by hand. It is sized like the cover, and may have snaps or Velcro closures. Choose a pocket with Velcro closures for diaper that will be primarily used by other care givers.

For pad folding instructions, look in the folding section of this book. How to prepare a pocket diaper:

• Stuff the appropriately sized folded diaper into the pocket (between the outside cover and the inner mesh).

• Smooth it out so it lies flat.

• Add a liner. You may want to tuck the end of the liner behind the pad in the back.

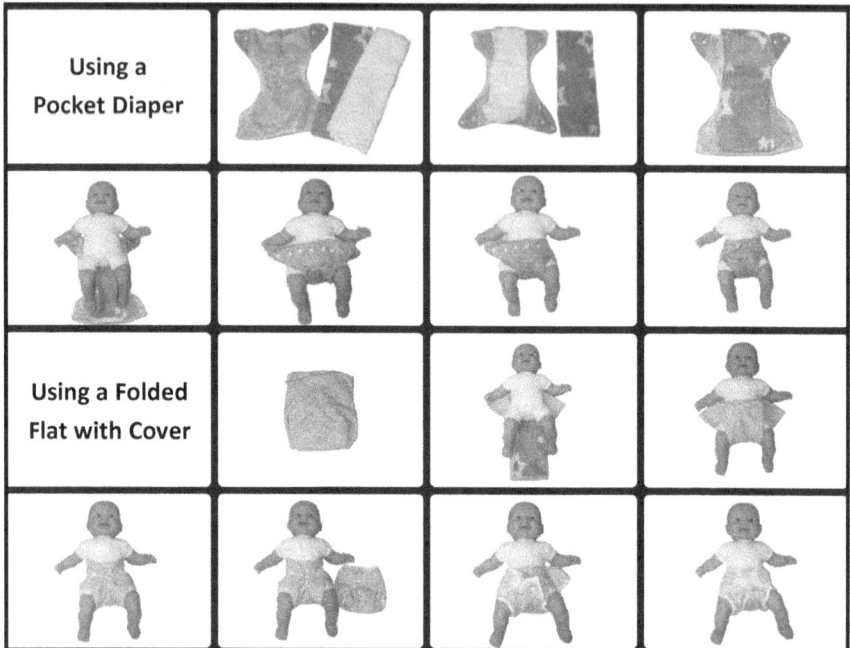

Using a Pocket Diaper			

Using a Folded Flat with Cover			

- Fold up the diaper, and it is ready to be used.

How to Put on a Cloth Diaper with a Cover

Changing a classic diaper is basically like changing a regular disposable, except that there is the added step of fastening the cover.

Putting a Classic Diaper
on a Naked Baby

- Open diaper and liner.
- Raise baby's bottom and slide diaper under her.
- Pull front of diaper between her legs.
- Overlap the wings at the waist.
- Pin or Snappi in place.
- Unfold cover.
- Raise baby's bottom and slide cover under her.
- Pull front of cover between her legs.

• Use Velcro tabs to secure at the waist.

This may seem more difficult than it actually is, as it generally takes less than a minute to complete all of these steps, even after a bath! Changing a baby that is already wearing a cover is much faster.

Changing the Diaper

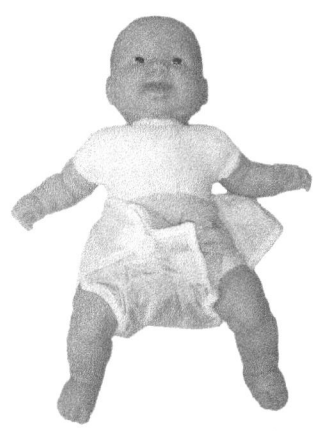

• Unhook Velcro sides.
• Pull down cover front.
• Unsnap the Snappi.
• Pull down diaper front
• If the baby is poopy, use front of diaper with liner to remove as much waste as you can.
• If the diaper is just wet, remove diaper, leaving cover in place under baby. Cover can be reused for three or four changes, as long as it isn't soiled. Rinse soiled cover and put to the side.
• Open diaper and liner.
• Raise baby's bum and slide diaper under her.
• Pull front of diaper between her legs.
• Overlap the wings at the waist.
• Pin or Snappi in place.

- Pull front of cover between her legs.
- Use Velcro tabs to secure at the waist.
- Shake off any solids on the liner into toilet.
- Place diaper, liner, and cloth wipes in wet bag/diaper pail.
- Wash every three to four days.

How to Use a Snappi

- Hold diaper in place with your non-dominant hand.
- Hook left hook to the left side.
- Hook the right hook to the right side.
- Hook the center hook to the crotch area...done!

How to Use Diaper Pins

- Open diaper pin.
- Put your hand between the baby and the diaper on the side you are going to pin.
- Poke pin in and up.
- Close and lock head.
- Repeat on the other side.

Using diaper pins takes practice, but it's good to have a few on hand just in case you lose or break your Snappis.

Sharp pins are safe pins. If you have to fight to get the pin through the cloth, you risk stabbing yourself sooner or later. A good diaper pin should slide through the cloth like a hot knife through butter.

You can keep your pins sharp by storing them with their points stuck in a block of soap.

Some people prefer pins over Snappis since it is very hard, if not impossible for a child to pull a diaper pin loose. With diaper pins, your child can go cover free.

Give HOPE

Here's what you can do to spread the word about *Rediscovering HOPE*:

1. Please like this book on Facebook www.facebook.com/HOPEDiapers

2. Please tweet about it on Twitter #HOPEDiapers

3. Send links to the download Rediscovering.HOPEDiapers.org

4. Consider purchasing copies of the brochure edition of this book for local charities, community service, family aid group at:
   http://hopediapers.org/get-booklets

The Art of Folding Classic Diapers

If you research flat diaper folds, you'll find over a dozen different types. However, we will only be looking at diaper folds that meet two essential criteria:

1. Can Be Folded in Advance. This is important, as it allows any caregiver to get onboard right from the get-go. If you fold up all your diapers at one time, after they are washed, they will be ready to grab and used by anyone who needs to change the baby. Once a flat diaper is folded, it is no harder to use than any other cloth diaper.

2. Limits the Number of Places Poop can go. If you need to wash diapers by hand for whatever reason, this is important. Some folds will keep runny baby poop in one section of the diaper, others don't.

On the next page you'll find a list of some of my favorite folds as well as details about how they each meet the above criteria.

Fold Name	Grab & Go	Contains Poop	Fastener	Layers - Back/ Middle/Front	Layers-Sides
Jo's fold	Yes	Yes	Snappi, Pins	2/6/6	2
Kite Fold	Yes	Yes	Snappi, Pins	5/5/12	3
Gaynor's fold	No	Yes	Tie or wrap	6	2
Neat Fold	Yes	Yes	Snappi, Pins	4/4/10	3
Neater Fold	Yes	Yes	Snappi, Pins	4/4/10	3
HOPE Fold	Yes	Yes	Snappi, Pins	6/9/10	3
Pad Fold	Yes	No	Not Used	12	0

Jo's Fold

This fold makes a thirty-inch square small enough to fit a tiny newborn without being too bulky, because the layers are evenly spread. (See tips below for reducing the size of a flat for newborns/small babies.)

1. Fold left and right corner to the center. The more you overlap the corners, the smaller the final diaper will be.

2. Fold up bottom corner, overlapping as needed.

3. Fold down the top corner. Overlap the sides and bottom a little. This will ensure that the majority of poop stays on one panel rather than getting all over the diaper.

4. Fold into thirds, like the pad fold.

5. Holding the middle side where the flap is, put out the left and right wing.

6. Lay fleece liner down the center.

7. Bring the bottom up to the top edge.

8. Pull out wings and wrap around.

9. If not using immediately, lay facedown.

Kite Fold

This fold is good when you need to boost absorbency but Jo's fold is too bulky between your child's legs.

1. Imagine that there is a diagonal line running from the top left to the bottom right corner of the flat.

2. Fold the bottom left and top right corners to the center to meet the imaginary line.

3. Fold the bottom right corner up as far as you need to, according to your baby's size.

4. Fold the top left corner down to cover it all. This is your poop protection panel. (See above.)

5. Repeat Steps 4 through 9 of Jo's fold.

Folding Tip:

Stack and smooth all your diapers, liners, and pad-folded diapers if using to add extra absorbency without extra bulk. Fold diapers on the stack. Add extra absorbency and/or liners as you are folding.

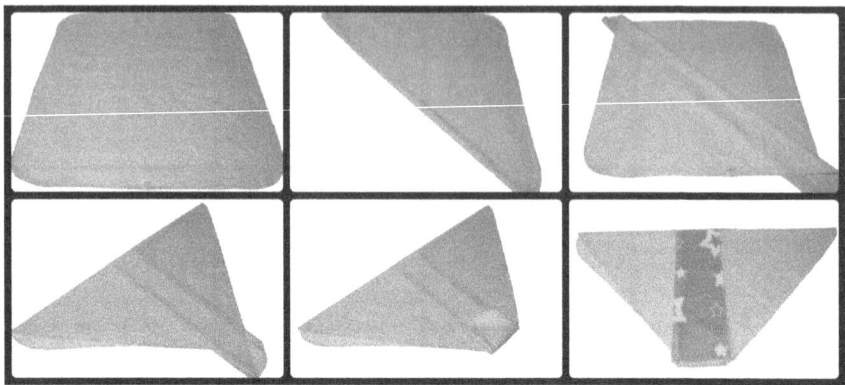

Gaynor's Fold

This fold gives some extra layers. It's great to know in a pinch, especially if you have misplaced your Snappis or pins. The wings are long so they can be tied or tucked around a baby and held on with the cover. You can adjust the wing length depending on the width of the pad that is created in the center.

1. Fold your flat diagonally, bringing the bottom left corner about an inch or two beyond the top right corner.

2. Bring the bottom left corner back over, leaving one to two inches width of three layers of fabric running diagonally from top left to bottom right.

3. Fold diaper in half diagonally, this time bringing the top left corner down to meet the bottom right.

4. If using a liner, lay it down the center.

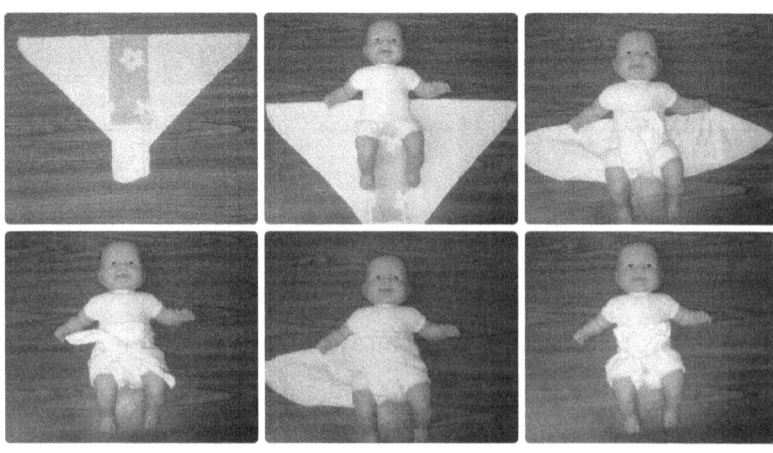

Neat Fold

This is a very simple and straightforward fold. You'll definitely want to use a liner so not to run the risk of getting poop on the edges. If you have to hand wash, that can prove to be a real pain.

1. With a corner of the diaper near you, fold the top and bottom corners toward the center. The top edge should be wider than the bottom. The bottom edge should be three times wider than the finished width of the diaper. How far you fold the two edges and how much they overlap will control the size of the diaper.

2. Fold the left and right corners to meet in the middle of the top edge.

3. Repeat Steps 4 through 9 of Jo's fold.

Tip: Folded diapers can be stored in a drawer, basket, box, or plastic storage bin.

Neater Fold

This is the same fold as above, just done in a different order to create a poop protection panel that will cover the majority of the diaper. It is neater in that you have less of a mess to wash.

1. With a corner of the diaper near you, fold the bottom corner toward the center. This edge should be three times wider than the finished width of the diaper.

2. Fold the left and right corners to meet in the middle.

3. Fold the top corner down to cover the rest.

4. Repeat Steps 4 to 9 of Jo's fold.

HOPE Fold

You can't fold hundreds of diaper without coming up with some of your own ideas. So here is my contribution to the world of flat diaper folds. It is a cross between the Gaynor's fold and the Neater fold. It works best for smaller babies, if using a Snappi fastener. For older babies or toddlers, you'll need to use pins or start with a larger flat.

1. Fold your flat diagonally, bringing the bottom left corner about an inch or two beyond the top right corner.

2. Bring the bottom left corner back over, but there should be a one- to two-inch width of three layers of fabric running diagonally from top left to bottom right.

3. Fold the bottom right corner up toward the center. The bottom edge should be about three times wider than the finished width of the diaper.

4. Fold the left and right corners/sides to touch the sides of the center pad.

5. Fold the upper left corner down to cover the rest

6. Repeat Steps 4 through 9 of Jo's fold.

Standard Pad Fold

This is the simplest of all of the diaper folds. It can be used alone, inside a diaper cover, or inside another folded diaper as a booster or for extra overnight protection.

1. Fold diaper in half.
2. Fold diaper in half again.
3. You now have a smaller square.
4. Fold the square into thirds.
5. Lay in cover or add to another diaper as booster.

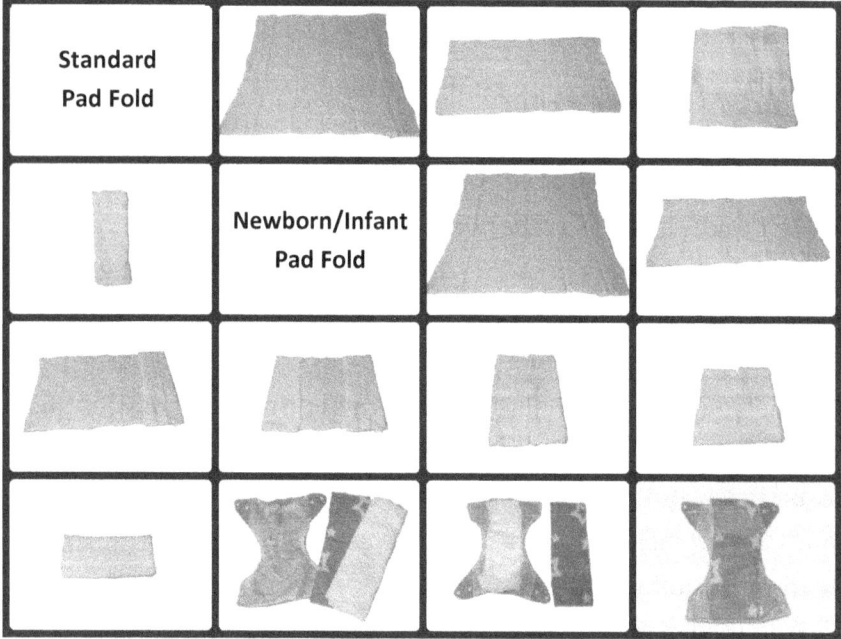

Standard Pad Fold			
	Newborn/Infant Pad Fold		

Newborn/ Infant Pad Fold
(from Zepher Hill blog)

1. Fold diaper in half.
2. Fold the left and right sides a quarter of the way in.
3. Fold the left and right sides in to the middle.
4. Fold up from the bottom into thirds.

Sizing / Absorbency Tips:

- You can make a smaller square for a newborns or very small infants by folding the right side and bottom up a few inches before starting the fold.
- You can make best use of the extra folded in material in any diagonal fold by turning the diaper so the two folded sides are at the bottom of the diaper.
- For nighttime, naptime, older babies, or heavy wetters, you may need to fold more than one flat together as one or add a pad-folded flat to the wet zone as you are folding.

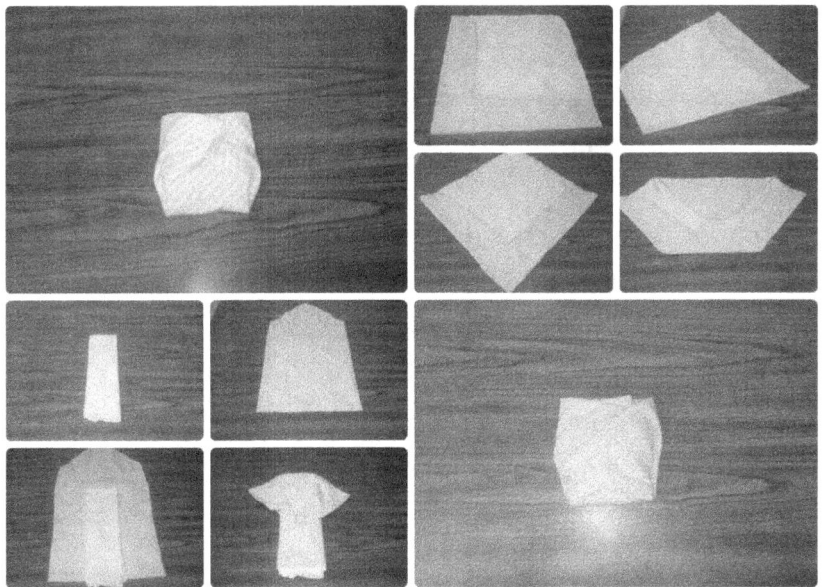

Washing Diapers

Washing diapers can be as simple or as complicated as you want. My advice? Try to keep things simple!

Less may be more in some aspects of life, but this is not true with diapers. You need to change your child(ren) when they are wet/poopy. This is best for their skin and will lead to better habits when they get older. This will also keep your diapers from becoming overly saturated with urine.

It really is important to have a minimum of thirty-six diapers on hand or the equivalent of four days' worth, whichever is more. Unless you just enjoy living on the edge, you want enough diapers to be able to wash every three to four days without running out of clean diapers when you are doing the wash.

Here is a basic washing routine that will work whether you wash by hand or in a washing machine:

• Sort poopy liners from rest of wash. (Optional)

• Soak/rinse diapers in plain cold water to remove the majority of pee and any residual poop.

• HOT wash with about one-quarter of the amount of cloth-friendly detergent. (See below.)

• Rinse.

• Rinse again

• Dry.

And that's it!

The above steps can be applied to a variety of laundry situations, as below.

Sort Poopy Liners (Optional)

When you change your child, make a conscious effort to use the liner-covered front of the diaper to wipe poop before you grab a baby wipe to finish the job. At washing time, just pull the liners out as you are unfolding the diapers to toss them in a bucket of water to soak. Agitate and rinse the liners to remove the majority of mess before adding them to the regular load. Using a device like the Breathing Mobile Washer make this a lot less messy.

Soak/Rinse

This is a very important step. I've tried washing routines that skip this step and go straight to a cold wash, and I've found that our daughter's diapers don't get as clean. This is especially important if you store your diapers dry (recommended) and not in water.

To do this, basically fill up your washer (tub/large storage bin,

if you are hand washing) and just grab a corner and open the diapers up. This ensures that the whole diaper will be exposed to water.

If I'm washing in a large storage bin in my tub, I'll grab my Breathing Mobile Washer and agitate the diapers, let them sit, then come back and agitate them some more. When the water changes color, I dump the diapers in a laundry basket with lots of holes or a storage crate to let the excess water drain off. I press the diapers against the sides to help remove the majority of water, but I do not wring the diapers.

If you are using an HE washer, this step is a little different. You'll toss your opened diapers into the machine and set it to wash on delicate; this option uses the most water.

Wash/Rinse/Rinse

Do a hot wash. If washing by hand use about one-quarter to one-half the amount of cloth-friendly detergent. If washing in a machine use the manufactures recommended amount. (See below.) Rinse the diapers at least twice. If you can see soap bubbles/froth or feel detergent residue, rinse again.

Dry

If you live in the country, consider line drying. If not, you can toss the diapers in the dryer. Flats dry incredibly fast, much faster than any other type of diaper. See the tips below for speeding up the process.

Washing Tips and Tricks

Since the beginning, I've tested out a variety of hand washing techniques. I've had the opportunity to try flat cloth diaper washing methods in a variety of washing machines as well. I own an HE front-loader and two mini washing machines. I also purchase and ended up returning a top-loading, pulsating washing machine. I've washed multiple loads in all of the above, so I will share with you what I've learned.

General Washing Tips

• There is no need to rinse your diapers in the toilet. Most poop will be caught on the liner. For "peanut butter poop," get a cheap spatula and mark it "Diapers" with a Sharpie. Store it in a container by the toilet and use it to scrape stubborn solids into toilet. Any other rinsing can be done in the bathroom sink.

• Don't wash more than thirty-six flat diapers at a time. If you overload your wash machine, none will get thoroughly clean.

• Use one-quarter of the amount of detergent when washing. If the diapers are really messy, use one-half. You may need to use more detergent if your water is hard.

• Use only hot water for the wash. This will prevent buildup that can lead to smelly diapers or diaper rash.

• If you can, hang your diapers in the sun, a natural disinfectant and brightener. Drying wet diapers in the sun will help to remove stubborn stains and whiten them without using bleach (another diaper no-no).

• Your baby is part of your family, so their poop is safe for your family. There is no need to disinfect the wash machine after you've washed the diapers. The presoak, wash, and double-rinse more than takes care of any residual poop.

Washing in Machines:

• Any type of top-loading, pulsating, agitator-free washer should be avoided with flats. The back-and-forth washing action ties the diapers into knots and causes an unbalanced load. The diapers must be untangled and readjusted after each cycle. Regular top-loading washers with center agitators are fine.

• HE washers conserve water, but this is not great for getting diapers clean. You'll need to trick your machine into using more water for at least the first rinse cycle. This can be done in the following ways: 1) Use the delicate wash cycle; 2) Add a water-soaked bath towel; and 3) Pour extra water though the place where you add detergent, though this may void your warranty.

• In my personal opinion, mini washers are not worth the stress and effort if you have more than a few items to wash. If you have to go the route of a nonconventional, portable washing machine, the Breathing Mobile Washer really is the best and most efficient, especially when the other option doesn't offer set

-it-and-forget-it options.

Washing by Hand

• As far as possible, try to do everything in loads. If you are soaking, soak everything. If you are washing, wash everything. You'll use less water and will also avoid burnout. Washing a lot of little loads will make you feel as if you are not accomplishing much.

• Use a plastic laundry basket or a crate with holes in it to drain the diapers. Let gravity help you with the water removal, as

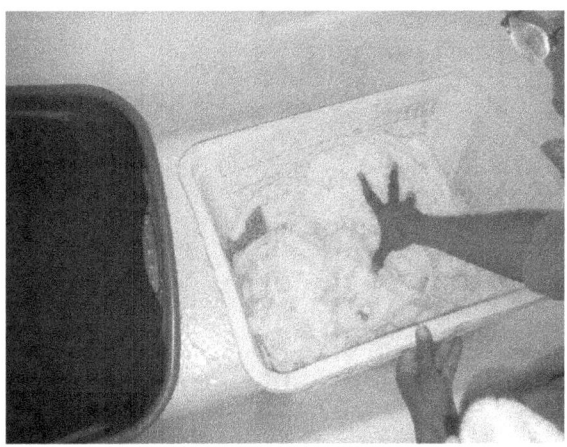

it will save your hands.

• Only wring out the last load.

•Start off with one-quarter the amount of soap and add more if needed. This is much easier than adding too much, which will require more rinsing.

• If you can afford it, invest in a laundry spinner. It will save your wrist and arms, and your diapers will dry fast: one to two hours inside, one hour on the line on a breezy day, and fifteen minutes in a hot dryer.

• Put on some music or listen to the radio, TED talks, the Bible or a class while you're washing. It will make the time go by faster and relax you or allow you to do something constructive in the meantime.

• Don't make it too complicate or draw it out. Set your mind on doing it and just knock it out. More than 50 percent of the world wash their clothes by hand, most without running water or cool tools. It isn't that big of a deal.

Detergent to Use

One of the most important aspects of taking care of your diapers is the type of detergent you use. Here are some mainstream

detergents that will work:
- All Free and Clear
- All Small and Mighty
- Arm & Hammer Essentials Free
- Arm & Hammer Sensitive Skin
- Purex Free and Clear
- Sun Free
- Sunlight Ultra Sensitive Skin
- Sunlight Ultra Sensitive Skin HE
- Tide Free
- Woolite HE

Things to Avoid

It is best to avoid any laundry products that contain the following:
- Enzymes (may cause rashes on sensitive skin)
- Fabric softeners
- Stain guards
- Natural oils
- Brighteners
- Perfumes
- Dyes

Diaper-Specific Detergents

A good number of detergents are specifically made for cloth diapers or work exceptionally well with them. Unfortunately, most can only be purchased online or at select stores. However, it may be worth the difficulty to find them, for you may find that they will work better than mainstream detergents.

Daddies, Daycares and Diapering

Flat diapers are often written off as not being a daddy-friendly cloth diaper option, but they don't have to be.

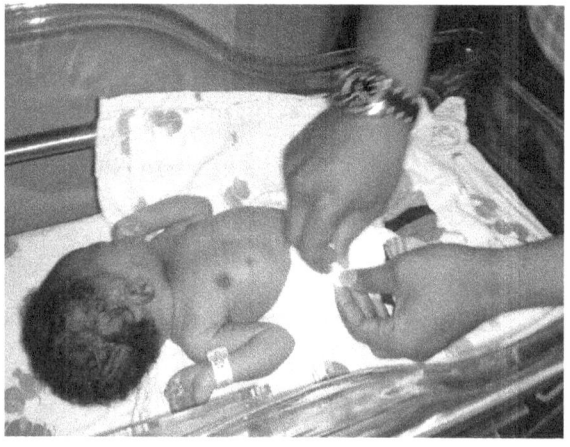

Daddies and Classic Cloth Diapers

My husband was open to using cloth in general, the t-shirt diapers in particular, since they only cost one dollar to make. When the t-shirt diapers didn't fit, I folded the flour sack towels, and he didn't miss a beat. He was changing our daughter's diapers in the hospital right from the beginning and changes his fair share of cloth diapers every day. If the ease of use didn't win him over, the savings did. He's a true believer now!

Here's my summary of how you can help your significant other find HOPE in flats:

- Make using flat cloth diapers easy. Make sure to keep them folded and ready. If s/he wants to learn to fold them too, great! But be happy if they are just willing to use them.

- Give them their own stash and don't touch it. This is for them to use when they can't find diapers and you aren't around to make any.

- Consider the principles for providing a happy daycare experience below. The same apply to providing good experiences for other family members.

Daycare-Friendly Classic Diapering

Most daycare facilities will not use a two-part diapering system, but they can still use flat diapers. You only have to make it as easy for them as possible.

I've personally called and spoken to a dozen or so childcare facilities in the city where I live. Those I spoke with either misunderstand the Department of Health rules regarding the use of cloth diapers in a daycare setting or think they will be asked to use pins and plastic pants and have to swish poopy diapers in the toilet.

When providers learn that there are no state or local rules against cloth diapers in daycare setting and that there are actually guidelines for uses, many are open to taking a second look. When they see that modern cloth diapers can be used almost as simply as disposables and can be stored in a wet bag and sent home with a child at the end of the day like any other piece of soiled clothing, many are willing to work with cloth diapering parents.

Keep the following in mind when working with a childcare provider who has stated a wiliness to serve with parents who use cloth diapers.

Any childcare provider who is willing to work with you is doing you a favor. Although, in most states, there are no rules against using cloth diapers in daycare settings, there is nothing stating that a childcare provider has to allow it. It is their personal choice. Be respectful of that and do your best to make their experience with cloth as positive as possible. If you do, it is likely that other parents who use cloth will have an easier time finding facilities that are open to using it.

Here are a few things you can do to create a positive experience for your daycare provider:

• **Use pocket diapers.** They are easier and more familiar than folded flats and covers. Most providers will not reuse a diaper cover once it has been on a child, even if it has not been soiled. Send your pre-stuffed and lined diapers, and everyone will be happier.

• **Provide them with an adequate supply of pocket diapers (four to six diapers per day) with some disposables for backup.** Unless you have purchased enough pocket diapers for at least a day and a half, you may need to supplement the daycare stash with disposables. If you understand this, it will save you stress when you don't have time to wash and save your daycare provider the stress of not having enough diapers for your child.

• **Do NOT ask or expect them to dump or rinse poopy diapers.** The most any provider can do is shake formed solids into the toilet. If you find someone who will do that, it's great for them and you. Don't expect it and you won't be disappointed.

Making classic cloth diapering accessible to daddies and daycare just boils down to making it easier for them to work with you. Changing a cloth diaper is really no different than changing a disposable. You just throw the dirty one in a pail at home or a wet bag instead of in the trash. Keep it sweet and simple, and everyone will be happy.

Give HOPE

Here's what you can do to spread the word about *Rediscovering HOPE*:

1. Please like this book on Facebook www.facebook.com/HOPEDiapers

2. Please tweet about it on Twitter #HOPEDiapers

3. Send links to the ebook Rediscovering.HOPEDiapers.org

4. Consider purchasing bulk copies of the informational brochure edition of this book for local charities, community service, family aid group at: http://HOPEdiapers.org/

Solving Problems in Paradise

So, you are enjoying your new, super affordable, wonderfully green cloth diapering system when trouble strikes. Don't worry! I've got you covered.

Leaky Diaper Syndrome

This is actually a very common problem for new cloth diaper users. There are a few easy-to-make mistakes that cause it.

Did you remember to prewash/prep?

Out of the package, any 100 percent cotton flat cloth may absorb some wetness, but they are not going to be as close to as absorbent as they would be if you prepped them (washed or boiled). These will not reach full absorbency until they've been used and washed five or six times.

Is the diaper/cover the right size? Is there a snug fit around the baby's legs and waist?

It should be snug enough that no diaper shows in the openings but loose enough to get a finger between the leg or waist opening.

Is all of the diaper tucked in?

If there is any bit of diaper sticking out of the leg or waist, it will allow moisture to leak out. Also, be careful not to tuck your child's clothing into the diaper.

Have you used any diaper creams without a liner?

Diaper creams can greatly affect the absorbency of your diapers. If you must use diaper creams, remember to use a liner and wash them separately from the diapers or use a disposable liner (Viva paper towels work) and throw it away.

Coconut oil is nourishing to the skin and is cloth diaper friendly. It can be found in the baking section of most grocery stores.

Is the baby being changed often enough?

Any kind of diaper will leak if it is left on too long. Changing babies often reduces the risk of diaper rash and keep their skin healthy. Newborns and infants should be changed every one to two hours when awake and every time they poop. Older children go less often, so the changes can be spaced farther apart.

Are you using natural detergents with built-in softener, fabric softeners, or dryer sheets?

These are a cloth diapering no-no. They will leave a coating on your diaper that will decrease the absorbency and can also be irritating to your baby's skin.

Stinky Diaper Syndrome

Do your diapers reek of ammonia as soon as your baby pees?

Even if your diapers smell clean from the wash, if they smell awful when they are wet, it means urine crystals are trapped in the fibers. This can happen when a diaper is saturated with pee and/or because the diapers are not being washed and rinsed in enough water. Unchecked, this can cause diaper rash.

Change your baby when she is wet. This is good for your baby, will prevent leaks, and will keep your diapers from marinating in pee until wash day.

Don't overload your washer. You want a full load but don't wash more than twenty-four to thirty-six diapers. If you are using an HE washing machine use the tips in the washing section to trick it into adding more water.

Do your diapers or covers stink and look dirty?

You probably have a buildup of detergent residue. To remove this, you'll need to wash your diaper several times in hot water with no detergent, until there are no suds in the water.

If there is no suds to start with, your covers are dirty. You need to use more detergent to wash them.

NOTES:

- http://pediatrics.aappublications.org/content/early/2013/07/23/peds.2013-0597.abstract
- http://manhattan.ny1.com/content/pages/136289/high-cost-of-diapers-forces-some-parents-into-risky-practices
- Wikipedia contributors, "Diaper," Wikipedia, The Free Encyclopedia, http://en.wikipedia.org/w/index.php?title=Diaper&oldid=576685171 (accessed October 11, 2013).
- Floursacktowels's Blog, "A Brief American History of the Flour Sack Towel. "Last modified 1 26, 2010. Accessed October 11, 2013. http://floursacktowels.wordpress.com/category/history-of-the-flour-sack-towel/.
- http://www.thetowelplace.com/merchant2/merchant.mvc?Screen=CTGY&Category_Code=FLFST
- http://www.diaperjungle.com/detergent-chart.html

Helpful Resources

Get HOPE Classic Cloth Diapering Kits and Supplies

I've created low-cost kits to help you get started. The HOPE Classic Cloth Diapering Kits includes the exact items that I use on my child and have referenced in the book as well as some helpful extras:

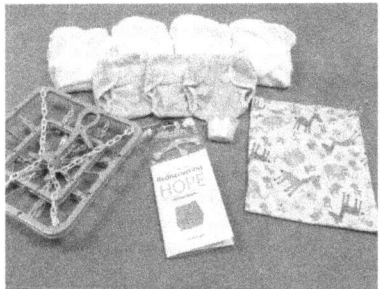 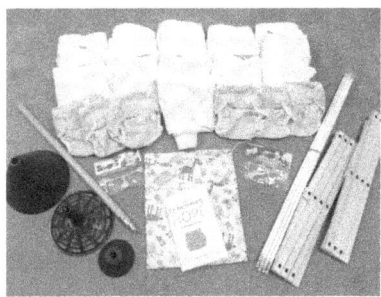

To complete the kit, you'll need to add 36 to 72 flat cloths (30"x30") of your choosing. These could be flour sack towels, receiving blankets, 100 percent flannel sheets cut to size with the edges finished, etc.

For more information or to order online or by mail visit HOPEDiapers.org.

Other Cloth Diapering Supplies

The following online retailers offer the supplies and items mentioned in this booklet in a variety of styles and at a variety of price points.

www.abbyslane.com

www.clothdiaperoutlet.com

www.cottonbabies.com

www.diaperjunction.com

www.diapersafari.com

www.jilliansdrawers.com

www.kellyscloset.com

www.nickisdiapers.com

www.sweetbottomsbaby.com

Hand Washing Supplies

Breathing Mobile Washer can be purchased from HOPEDiapers.org.

www.compactappliance.com sells the Mini Countertop Spin Dryer at the best price I've found online, with free shipping. They also seem to be more reliable than purchasing from the manufacture's site.

Book

Changing Diapers by Kelly Wels will give you more of a complete overview of ALL the various diapering options in the cloth diapering world. She is the founder and owner of DiaperShops.com and Kelly's Closet.

Blogs, Website, Forums

There are way too many to mention. For ongoing advice, encouragement, and support with flat cloth diapering, visit HopeDiapers.org. There, you'll find an up-to-date list of the various blogs, sites, and forums supportive of classy affordable cloth diapering.

About Me

Hi. My name is Amy McKnight.

I'm a wife, a mother, a friend, a designer, a seamstress, a presenter, a writer, a teacher, a thrifty, a do-it-yourselfer, socially conscious, service-driven, ministry minded, work-outside-the-home, classic cloth diapering mom.

What I've shared in this booklet comes from over a year's worth of research, trial and error, and personal experience. I drink my own Kool-Aid and eat my own pudding! I am doing exactly what I share in this booklet, because it works.

www.ingramcontent.com/pod-product-compliance
Lightning Source LLC
Chambersburg PA
CBHW070332290526
45791CB00003B/1310